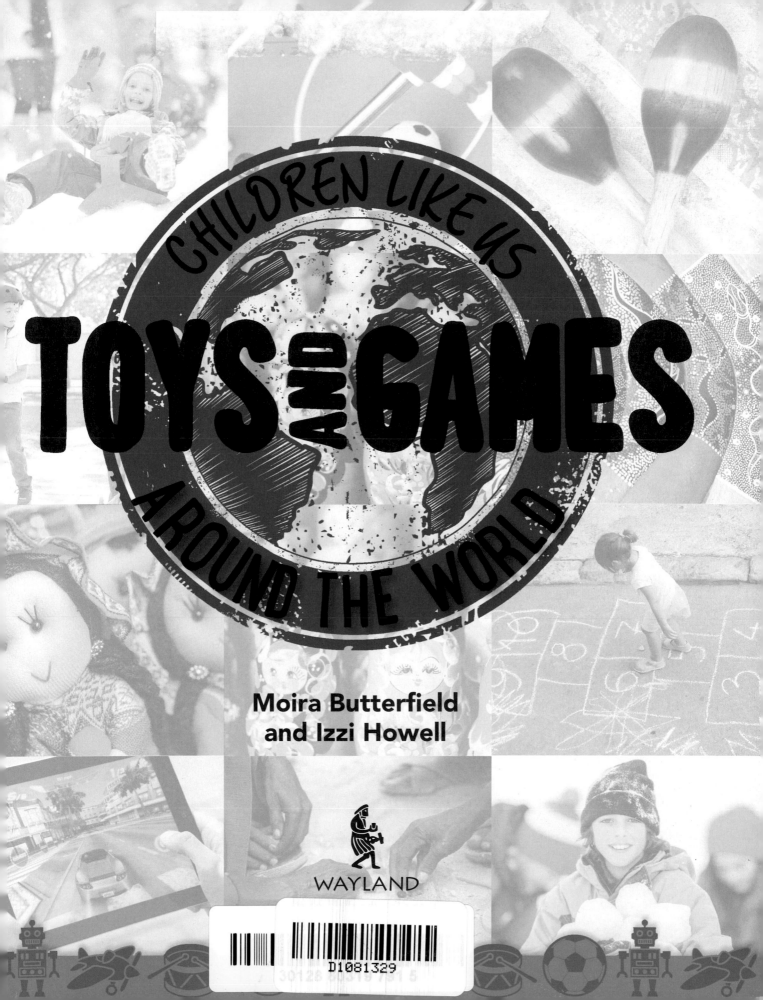

CHILDREN LIKE US

TOYS AND GAMES

AROUND THE WORLD

**Moira Butterfield
and Izzi Howell**

WAYLAND

Published in paperback in 2017
by Wayland

© Hodder and Stoughton, 2017

All rights reserved.

ISBN: 978 0 7502 9716 5

10 9 8 7 6 5 4 3 2 1

Wayland
An imprint of
Hachette Children's Group
Part of Hodder & Stoughton
Carmelite House
50 Victoria Embankment
London EC4Y 0DZ

An Hachette UK Company
www.hachette.co.uk
www.hachettechildrens.co.uk

Printed in China

Produced for Wayland by
White-Thomson Publishing Ltd
www.wtpub.co.uk

Editor: Izzi Howell
Designer: Clare Nicholas
Proofreader: Izzi Howell
Picture researcher: Izzi Howell
Wayland editor: Annabel Stones

Picture credits:

Contents

All Kinds of Toys and Games

Are you ready to travel around the world and see some of the different toys that children have and the games that they play? Join them playing sports and board games, making homemade toys and playing with dolls.

Some toys are made for the snow. Learn about these Canadian snow tubes on page 10.

It can be fun to build your own electronic toys. What do you think these American children are building? Find out on page 18.

In cities, children draw their own games on the pavement. Learn about this Polish girl's street game on page 6.

Toys can be handmade. What material is this Filipina girl weaving her toy from? Find out on page 20.

Different board games are played all over the world. Discover the Tanzanian game of Bao on page 14.

Take a journey around the world to discover the toys and games of children just like you!

City Games

Cities are crowded and busy but children find places to play in parks, squares and quiet streets. Even pavements can become a playground if you have some chalk to draw with.

Hopscotch is a great game to play on a pavement. You can draw a number grid and hop along it, like this Polish girl has done.

This circular hopscotch game is called escargot, which means 'snail' in French. To play escargot, you have to hop around the circle on one leg, jumping over the dotted squares.

This streetball hoop isn't attached to the ground, so it can be moved to different areas of the city.

Ball games are a good way to play in small city spaces where there isn't much room. These boys are playing streetball in the city of Volgograd, Russia. Streetball is a simple version of basketball, with just a few players practising their moves and having fun.

Children all around the world play clapping games in the street. These American girls are singing a rhyming song called 'Mary Mack' and clapping their hands in time to the music. The words to clapping songs are different in every country, but many of the clapping patterns are the same.

There are many movements in the American clapping song 'Mary Mack', such as clapping your right hand to your partner's right hand, and slapping your thighs.

Countryside Playtime

Living far away from towns doesn't mean there's nothing to play with. Instead of playgrounds and toyshops, there might be handmade and recycled toys to play with. These Ethiopian children are having fun with a wheel recycled from an old car.

An old wheel can become a toy to spin along and chase, as these Ethiopian children have found.

These children are from the Aborigine community in the Australian outback. They are playing with a boomerang carved from local wood. If they throw their boomerang in the right way, it will fly in a circle and come back to them.

Boomerangs were designed for hunting animals in the outback, but they make great toys, too.

The curved shape of a boomerang helps it to fly in a circle.

In Nepal, everyone in the village works together to build a ping swing for the children to enjoy.

In the village of Ghorepani, Nepal, the children get a great new toy once a year. It is a 'ping swing', made from bamboo poles and grass ropes. It's built as part of a yearly Hindu religious festival called Dashain, celebrated in September or October.

Fun in the Snow

Snowballs are too cold to hold in your bare hands, so this Swedish boy is wearing insulated gloves.

There's only one rule in a snowball fight – if you are hit, you are out! However, it is so much fun to make and throw snowballs that most games don't follow this rule.

In the past, sledges were used as a form of transport, but nowadays they make a great toy. Traditionally, sledges were made of wood, but this Norwegian girl is using a plastic version. Some modern sledges are even designed to do 'snow surfing' stunts.

This Norwegian sledge has a handle to help with steering.

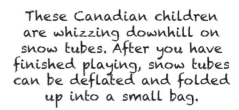

These Canadian children are whizzing downhill on snow tubes. After you have finished playing, snow tubes can be deflated and folded up into a small bag.

This photo was taken by someone jumping high above the blanket. In the past, the blanket was made of sealskins, but now it is usually made from canvas.

Inuit communities in Alaska and Canada often play the traditional game of 'blanket toss' at the Nalukataq spring festival. The blanket is used as a trampoline – the players tug around its edges to make the person on it bounce up and down.

Wonderful Water Toys

On a hot day, it's fun to cool down with water. In Florida, USA, the city of West Palm Beach puts up a giant water slide every summer for children to play on. Most children slide down on an inflatable pool toy for extra speed!

This city water slide in the USA is over 300m long!

At the Thai New Year's festival of Songkran, it's traditional to pour water on other people as it is thought to wash away bad luck. Thai children often celebrate Songkran by getting out their water pistols, and spraying each other in the street.

This Thai boy is ready to soak his friends with his water pistol as part of the Songkran festival.

You don't need to get wet to have fun with water. These boys are getting ready to sail their toy boat on the ocean near their home in Tanzania. Their handmade boat is made from recycled pieces of wood and plastic, held together by string.

The extra pieces of wood attached to the sides of the boat will help it to float on the water.

Brilliant Board Games

The board game Bao is popular in East Africa. The aim of Bao is to spread your pieces, called seeds, around the board and make moves to take as many seeds from the other players as possible. The word 'bao' means 'board' in the Swahili language.

Although the pieces in Bao are called seeds, they can be pebbles, shells or even rolled up dung balls. These Tanzanian players are using pebbles.

Some board games have been played for many centuries, such as chess and the Chinese game of Go. Like chess players, Go players have either black or white pieces. They must move their pieces around, trying to cover the board with their colour.

These South African children are playing chess. Chess may have been invented in India, but it's such an old game that nobody knows for sure.

These Chinese children are playing Go. They must think ahead to plan their next move, like chess players.

This boy is using a Snakes and Ladders board designed for people with little or no sight. He can feel each square and the patterns on the board. The board also has pictures on it so that he can play a game with someone who can see.

This boy is using his fingers to sense holes and patterns on a game of snakes and ladders.

Making Music

Chinese rattle drums have small wooden balls hanging from either side. They rattle onto the drum when it is shaken. Maracas come from South America, where they have been used for over a thousand years. They have seeds inside them that make a noise when the maracas are shaken.

Maracas always come in pairs, one for each hand.

Around the stick of this Chinese rattle drums there is a paper dragon, symbolising good fortune.

This Brazilian boy is hitting this recycled plastic drum with his hands to create a rhythm.

You don't always need a musical instrument to make music. This Brazilian boy is using an old plastic container as a drum. His sister is holding a smaller container, which could also be used as a drum.

This Peruvian girl has her own set of South American pan pipes. Each little tube is made from a hollow reed of a different length. They will each make a different note when the girl blows over the top.

Pan pipes are a popular music toy all over South America.

Electronic Fun

The first robots were invented over 60 years ago. Today, you can buy remote-controlled robot toys, or even kits to build your own robot! These American children are working together to make a robot of their own. Some schools around the world even hold competitions for robot building.

Each child is putting together a different part of the robot toy.

With a mobile phone or a tablet, you can download thousands of game apps to play with. Some apps test your memory or knowledge, with difficult quizzes. Other apps allow you to race cars, look after a virtual pet or design your own town.

This tablet has a touch screen, so you can control the car in this racing game app by touching the screen.

These girls from the United Arab Emirates have their own computer games console in their bedroom.

There is only one games console for these Egyptian boys to share in this desert tent.

Computer games are popular all over the world. In some countries, children have their own games consoles at home. In other countries, games consoles are shared between many children, such as this group of friends in a desert oasis in Egypt. While two children play on the games console, their friends wait eagerly for their turn!

Homemade Toys

This girl from the Philippines is making a toy from palm leaves. She is weaving the leaves together to make a shape, like the fish shown here. It's possible to make all sorts of shapes from the leaves, including animals, dolls, hats and boxes.

This girl is weaving a toy from palm leaves that come from the countryside around her home.

This fish is made from woven palm leaves that have dried out.

The screen on this homemade Ethiopian TV toy changes when you turn the wooden handle at the bottom. Inside the wooden frame is a tiny roll of paper, which has drawings and words written on it to tell a story. When the handle is turned, the paper moves along inside the toy.

Ethiopian children can add their own drawings and stories to a homemade TV toy.

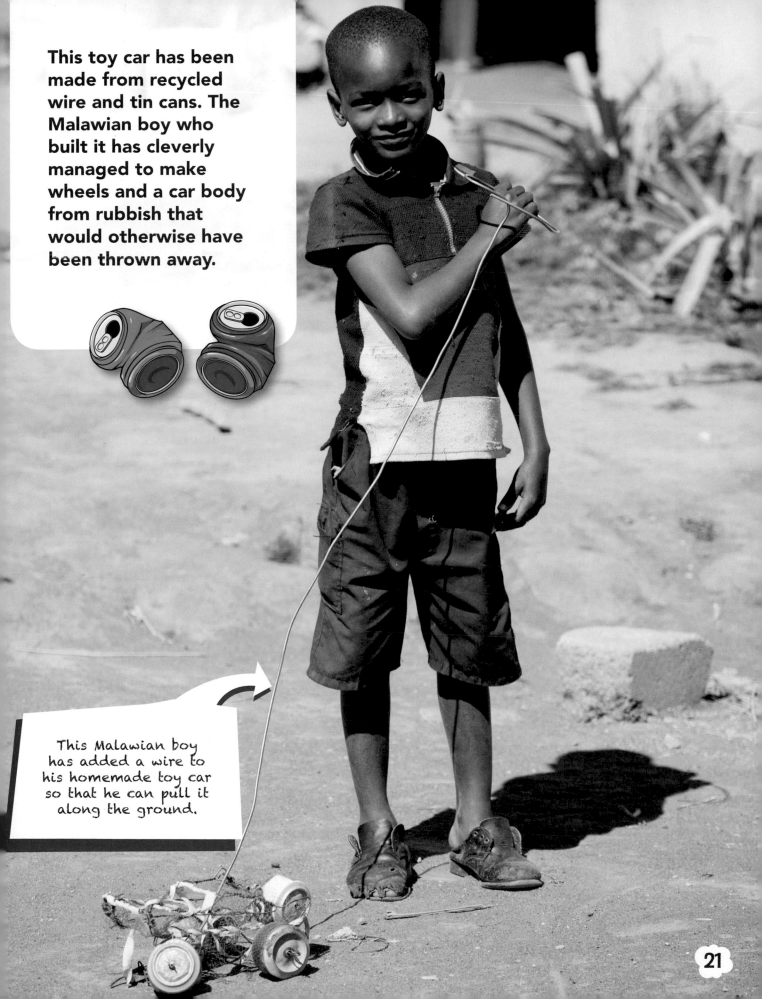

This toy car has been made from recycled wire and tin cans. The Malawian boy who built it has cleverly managed to make wheels and a car body from rubbish that would otherwise have been thrown away.

This Malawian boy has added a wire to his homemade toy car so that he can pull it along the ground.

All Sorts of Dolls

These worry dolls are made for children in Guatemala and Mexico. In these countries, children tell their worries to the dolls before they go to bed. Then they pop the dolls under their pillows, so that the dolls will take their troubles away during the night.

South American worry dolls are even given to children in hospitals to help them feel better about their stay.

It can be hard to make doll-sized items of clothing. This Lithuanian doll's headband is made from a thin ribbon.

Dolls often wear national costume. Lithuanian dolls wear traditional fabric belts and lace collars. Romanian dolls are often dressed in mini versions of the embroidered blouses and skirts that Romanian girls wear on national holidays.

These Romanian dolls have hair made from wool which is plaited in a traditional style.

Inside every Russian matryoshka doll is a set of smaller matching dolls! As you get further inside the matryoshka, the dolls get smaller and smaller. All the dolls are painted to look like they are wearing traditional Russian dresses and headscarves.

This girl is painting her own set of matryoshka dolls.

Traditionally, all the matryoshka dolls in a set are painted the same colours.

Super Sports

These Russian children are playing a game of street hockey in a city square. The curved ends of their hockey sticks make it easier for them to hit the ball. Hockey can also be played on ice, with all the players on ice skates.

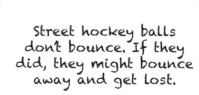

Street hockey balls don't bounce. If they did, they might bounce away and get lost.

It looks like this Indian batsman is going to hit the ball, but if he misses, the ball may hit the wickets and he will be 'out'.

All over India, you will see children playing cricket, the country's most popular sport. These children are practising on a field, using sticks as wickets. It's traditional to wear white clothes when you are playing cricket.

Football is the world's most popular sport, and children can be seen playing it with their friends in fields or streets around the world. Many of the world's greatest footballers started out playing football in the street with their friends, before becoming famous.

This South African boy is part of a football club that gives free football coaching to children from poor areas.

All Sorts of Wheels

This Spanish boy is trying out some ramps on his scooter at a park in Barcelona. To get up the ramp, he needs to push one of his feet against the floor, but going down the ramp is easy!

The first scooters were made from wooden boards and roller skate wheels. Nowadays, scooters are made from lightweight metal and they have larger wheels.

Not all bicycles have two wheels! This girl is learning how to ride a unicycle – a one-wheeled bicycle.

Bicycles were first invented over 200 years ago, and now children everywhere play and travel on them. These Thai children have an unusual version – a tandem bicycle for three! The littlest child in the family is sitting at the back and her big brother and sister are doing all the pedalling.

This tandem bicycle is perfect for a family or a group of friends to try out.

This Canadian boy is in a skate park, where skateboarders can play safely and try out their moves.

The first skateboarders were Californian surfers in the 1950s who wanted something to ride on when the waves were flat. In 1969, the first curved skateboard appeared and suddenly it was possible to control the board and do tricks. Skateboarding soon became a worldwide hit with children everywhere.

Flying Toys

A paper plane is one of the easiest toys to make for yourself. Most paper planes are made from a folded piece of paper, but in some areas, children make planes from folded palm leaves or recycled pieces of wood.

This boy has made a toy plane from thin wood. He is using an elastic band to launch it into the air.

This girl is getting ready to throw her paper plane into the air.

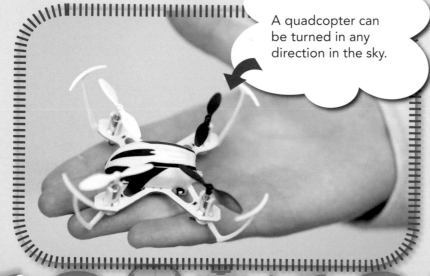

A quadcopter can be turned in any direction in the sky.

This tiny quadcopter has four rotating blades that help it to lift into the air and fly around. Inside the quadcopter, there are electric controls that allow you to fly and steer it from the ground.

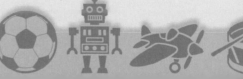

These Japanese kite fighters are using six-sided fighting kites called rokkaku.

This boy is flying a small, four-sided kite. This type of kite is usually used for kite fighting in Afghanistan.

Kite fighting is a popular sport in Afghanistan, Pakistan and southeast Asia. The aim of kite fighting is to cut the string of someone else's kite in the sky. This boy is practising with his kite near the city of Kabul, in Afghanistan. He will probably take part in kite fighting contests with his friends.

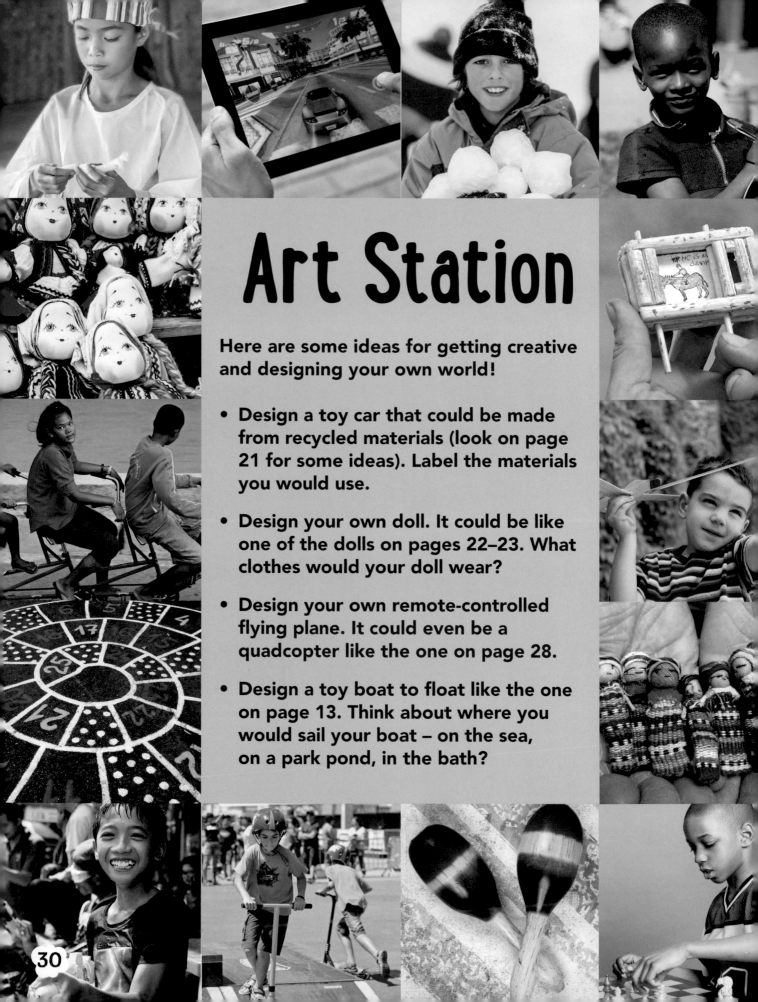

Art Station

Here are some ideas for getting creative and designing your own world!

- Design a toy car that could be made from recycled materials (look on page 21 for some ideas). Label the materials you would use.

- Design your own doll. It could be like one of the dolls on pages 22–23. What clothes would your doll wear?

- Design your own remote-controlled flying plane. It could even be a quadcopter like the one on page 28.

- Design a toy boat to float like the one on page 13. Think about where you would sail your boat – on the sea, on a park pond, in the bath?

Glossary

Aborigine a group of people who have lived in Australia for many centuries

community a group of people who live together

homemade made by hand, not in a factory

Inuit a group of people who live in the far north of North America

national costume clothes that are typical of a particular country

oasis a place in the desert where there is water

outback a vast countryside region in the middle of Australia, where few people live

palm a kind of tree that grows in areas where there is lots of warm weather

recycled used again, in a different way

remote-controlled controlled by radio signal

rotating something that turns in a circular direction

sense to feel something rather than see it

streetball a simple version of basketball

version an example of something

virtual something that exists on a computer, rather than in real life

further Information

Websites

A series of photos of children around the world with their favourite toys.
http://www.telegraph.co.uk/culture/photography/10729281/Toys-around-the-world.html

Information about toys and games around the world, organised by country.
http://multiculturalkidblogs.com/2014/12/08/20-toys-games-from-around-the-world/

Some examples of recycled toys from around the world.
http://www.streetplay.com/playfulworld/recycledtoys.shtml

Further Reading

Discover Countries series (Wayland, 2014)

Mapping A Country series Jen Green (Wayland, 2015)

My Holiday in Australia, Jane Bingham (Wayland, 2014)

Index